THE WORLD, THE CHURCH, AND THE PRIESTHOOD OF BELIEVERS

STEPHEN ESSILFFIE

WESTBOW
PRESS®
A DIVISION OF THOMAS NELSON
& ZONDERVAN

WestBow Press books may be ordered through booksellers or by contacting:

WestBow Press
A Division of Thomas Nelson & Zondervan
1663 Liberty Drive
Bloomington, IN 47403
www.westbowpress.com
844-714-3454

ISBN: 978-1-6642-7203-3 (sc)
ISBN: 978-1-6642-7204-0 (hc)
ISBN: 978-1-6642-7202-6 (e)

Library of Congress Control Number: 2022912750

Print information available on the last page.

WestBow Press rev. date: 5/11/2023

CONTENTS

To the Church of Pentecost,
the Leesburg Assembly, in Herndon, Virginia

DEDICATED TO LEESBURG ASSEMBLY

The Church of Pentecost, the Leesburg Assembly, in Herndon, Virginia, was opened on June 25, 2016, in an evening service, under the able leadership of Pastor Sampson Wilberforce Ohene. It started with a membership of fourteen. Elder and Mrs. Darfour were present as visitors. Also in attendance were Elder Stephen Ekuban Essilfie, Deacon Raymond Asigbee, and Deaconess Justina Adjoa Wirdua Brown.

As the Bible says, go into all nations, preach the word to those who will believe, baptize them, and teach them—that was what the pastor and his executives set out to do—and they achieved it.

The presiding elder of Manassas Assembly (now Overseer Mark Twumasi) gave the word that evening. Despite not a humble beginning, today the Leesburg Assembly membership is over fifty. Praise and honor be to God in the highest. Zachariah 4:10

I would like to take this opportunity to thank the presbytery of the Leesburg Assembly, especially Deacon Raymond

Asigbee and Deaconess Justina Adwoa Wiredua Brown, Pastor Wilberforce Sampson Ohene, and Mama Evylen Ohene.

I would also like to thank the following people:

- District Pastor Hendon
- Overseer Samuel Agnim Boateng
- Overseer Mark Twuasi Agyman and his wife
- Regional Apostle Augustus Martey Seminor and Mama Seminor
- Elder Nobel Dacosta
- Elder James Ofei of Manassas Assembly
- Elder Augustine Dua and his wife, Leticia—they are like family. God richly blessed them.

And may God bless you as you read this book.

FOREWORD

The World, The Church, The Priesthood Believers by Elder Stephen Ekuban Essilfie draws Christians attention to the current deteriorating and decaying state of the world we live in from the biblical point of view. He then challenges the Church and the Priesthood of Believers to arise and be the salt and the light of the world.

The author makes a comparison between the ancient world and our modern world. He reminds readers that in the ancient world life was simple and beautiful. There were no technological gadgets yet people were happy and satisfied. People enjoyed natural food stuffs and the beautiful natural environment. There was no environmental pollution or global warming. Deadly diseases and sicknesses were not common as we see today.

People lived in communal settings and warmly interacted and shared meals together. Children were trained to respect and offer help to any elderly person they met on the street. The author relates that there were no many churches or organized religions, yet people were more religious and God-fearing. In our today's world the opposite is true. The fear of God is on the decline. Many people have become less religious, rather money, wealth and fame have become their idols.

Elder Essilfie considers the New Testament concept of the Church; its powers and purpose in shaping the world in a right direction. He argues that the modern Church must be a city of refuge for the lost, the poor, the social outcasts and the hopeless.

Finally, he encourages priesthood believers to understand the biblical implications of the rapidly changing world, use their limited wisely, actively impact their communities, neighborhoods and places of work for Jesus Christ.

I wholeheartedly recommend this book to all. You will be inspired, challenged and blessed.

Apostle John O. Ofori
Ohio Regional Head
The Church of Pentecost U.S.A. Inc

Apostle John Ofori—he is currently the national secretary of the Church of Pentecost USA Inc., and regional apostle of Ohio State. I can describe him as a good shepherd, meaning that he tries to know his members. He goes to their level to understand their situations so he can address them properly. He is the people's man. I have known him since he was a pastor in Virginia before he was transferred to Japan and became an apostle and a seasonal speaker. He has given talks at many conferences. He is also a family man with a wife and children and has two books himself.

ACKNOWLEDGEMENT

I will give thanks to the Lord the God whose promises are amen. He says, commit your ways to me, and I will establish it. Yes, this is what the Lord can do.

Who would have thought that one day, I would have come this far—writing a book for you to read. Believe in God, and your life will be changed more than you ever expected.

The following song was written by Charles Wesley in 1739:

> Oh, for a thousand tongues to sing
> My great Redeemer's praise,
> The glories of my God and King,
> The triumphs of his grace.
>
> My gracious Master and my God,
> Assist me to proclaim,
> To spread through all earth abroad,
> The honors of thy name.
> Jesus! the name that charms our fears,
> That bids our sorrows cease;

'Tis music in the sinner's ears,
'Tis life, and health, and peace.

He breaks the power of canceled sin,
He sets the prisoner free;
His blood can make the foulest clean;
His blood availed for me.

He speaks, and listening to his voice,
New life the dead receive,
The mournful broken hearts rejoice,
The humble poor believe.

Hear him, ye deaf. his praise. ye dumb,
Your loosened tongues employ;
Ye blind, behold your Savior come.
And leap, ye lame, for joy.

Glory to God and praise and love.
Be ever, ever given;
By saints below and saints above
The church in earth and heaven.

I would like to salute some men of God that I have come
to know well:

- The late Prophet M. K. Yeboah and Apostle Dr. M.
  K. Ntumy were former chairmen of the Church of
  Pentecost, for ten good years each—men of God. A

song says, "He is great, he is great, everything written about him is great." How these people were called into office is a mystery and a wonder that I cannot explain. Apostle M. K. Ntumy's proverb is, "If you have dogs, why do you use a goat for hunting?"

- Apostle Onyame Tiase (may he rest in peace) helped me when I was presiding at New Achimota Assembly.
- Apostle (retired) S. K. Ansong.
- Church of Pentecost Prophet Anum, may he rest in peace.
- Apostle Emmanuel Owusu of the Church of Pentecost, Canada National Head.
- Apostle Sampson Ofori Yeadom.
- Pastor John Hagee of the Cornerstone Church in Texas.
- Current chairman of the Church of Pentecost, Apostle Eric Kwabena Nyamekye. Daddy, I salute you.
- The late Elder Eric Tetteh, the first presiding elder of Nii Boi Town Assembly. He was very much a man of God. He used to walk all the way from Nima Mamobi to Nii Boi Town and walked back, sometimes not once and not twice. May his soul rest in peace.

INTRODUCTION

You are the salt of this earth but, if the salt loses its flavor how, shall it be seasoned? It is then good for nothing. But to be thrown out and trampled underfoot by men.

You are the light of the world. A city that is set on a hill cannot be hidden, nor do they light a lamp and put it under a basket but, on a lampstand and it gives light to all who are in the house.

Let your light shine before men that they may see your good works and glorify your father in heaven.

—Matthew 5:13–16

The above quotation is from one of the teachings of Jesus called the beatitudes.

In Latin, the word for beatitude is *beatus* and in Greek is *mak*, and it means almost the same as in English—blessings, happy, fortunate, lengthy.

The consensus among both Christians and non-Christians is that the declarations made in the Sermon on the Mount are greater and stricter than the Ten Commandments, with regard to morals.

This mountain is said to be between Gennesaret and Capernaum on the northern shore of the Sea of Galilee. Capernaum is today called Nhum, which means "Nahum's village" in Hebrew. It was a fishing village established during the time of the Hasmoneans and had a population of about 1,500. Gennesaret was an important Bronze and Iron Age city that was mentioned in the Old Testament and New Testament and in the Epic of Aqhat, a myth from Ugarit (an ancient city in the area that is now Syria).

Matthew 7:26–27 gives a refreshing look at this saying, the conclusion, and its response from the disciples:

> But everyone who hears these sayings of mine and does not do them will be like a foolish man who built his house on the sand and rains descended, the flood came and the winds blew and beat on that house and fell. And great was its fall.

And so it was that when Jesus finished these sayings, the people were astonished at his teachings, for he taught them as one who had authority and not like the scribes.

If all believers, including you and me, would live according to Jesus's teachings, how beautiful our lives would be.

I believe these things are used as symbols, as we all know what salt can do in a home and what light brings to human life.

As the Resurrection of Christ Jesus brings hope to the world, so must his spirit coming into our lives bring a transformation to every home and every situation to represent the work of salt and light.

CHAPTER 1

THE WORLD

I am not here to discuss the underworld or any world above because I have never been there. I am here to talk about the world that is on planet earth.

What is the world? The Bible mentions the word *world* thirty-five times, and the first is in Psalm 93:1.

> The Lord reigns he is clothed with majesty the Lord is cloth he has girded himself with strength, surely the world is established so that it cannot be moved.

The last time the word *world* is mentioned is in Revelation 13:3.

And I saw one of his heads as it were wounded
to death and his deadly wound was healed.
And the world wounded after the beast.

The book of Genesis teaches us that God created heaven
and the earth and the fullness thereof, but is that the world? Is
the earth the world?

> The earth is the Lord's and all the fullness
> thereof. They that dwell therein for he hath
> founded it upon the sea and established it upon
> the floods. (Psalm 24:1–2)

Is this the world? If not, then what is and where is the world?
Now let's look at what makes the world. The world
comprises all the activities that go on under the sun and all
around the earth, both physically and spiritually.
Hebrews 11:3 says:

> Through faith, we understand that the worlds
> were framed by the word of God, so that the
> things which are seen were not made of things
> which are visible.

Please take note of the word *worlds* in this scripture means
more than one.
Ephesians 6 will tell you about the operation of spiritual
powers, principalities, and high powers that operate in

darkness. It goes on to tell us to put on the full armor of God so that we can withstand the forces of these entities.

God cursed the earth after the fall of Adam in the garden of Eden and all the fullness thereof. The creatures that Adam and Eve were controlling turned on them. The animals that they were to kill and eat turned to kill Adam and Eve and eat them. The sea was not made to kill human beings, but today, the sea is killing people.

The apostle John said that one day the sea will give up its dead because there will be a time to account for its work. In Revelation 20:13, the sea gave up the dead who were in it, and death and Hades delivered up the dead who were in them, and they were judged, each one according to his or her works.

After this, the apostle John said,

> And I saw "a new heaven and a new earth" for the first heaven and the first earth were passed away and there was no more sea. (Revelation 21:1)

> A time will come when no lion, tiger, or snake will kill any human, let alone eat them.

Now let's consider physical activities, such as cultural, traditional practices; nightclubs; tribal issues—every human activity that goes on under the sun and on earth. All these things that come together form the world.

The Eastern World

Eastern world, also known as the East or the Orient, is an umbrella term for various social structures, nations, and philosophical systems, which vary depending on the context. It most often includes at least part of Asia, or geographically, the countries and cultures east of Europe, the Mediterranean region and the Arab world, specifically in historical (pre-modern) context, and in modern times in the context of Orientalism.

It is often seen as a counterpart to the Western world, and correlates strongly to the southern half of the North–South divide.[1]

The Western World

The Western world, also known as the West, refers to various regions, nations, and states depending on the context, most often consisting of the majority of Europe, North America, and Oceania. The Western world is also known as the Occident, in contrast to the Orient or Eastern world.[2]

---

[1] "Eastern World," Wikipedia, https://en.wikipedia.org/wiki/Eastern_world.
[2] "Western World," Wikipedia, https://en.wikipedia.org/wiki/Western_world.

Part of this world identifies itself as the Western world according to its culture, heritage, social norms, ethical values, and traditional customs.

You can see how these groups of people identify themselves as being a world of their own. This is my explanation of the *world* means.

CHAPTER 2

THE ANCIENT WORLD AND ITS LIFESTYLES

Let's consider the ancient world—a period that I describe as the best and the worst. What really happened during this period?

The beauty of nature was seen in the mountains, rivers, waterfalls, and changes of the sky. Individuals could walk many miles without getting tired. The food was organic. Many sicknesses of today were not heard of in the ancient world.

The world did not know environmental pollution or global warming. Train, car, and airplane accidents did not occur. The only accidents may have been accidents on the farm, a tree falling on people and buildings, and so forth.

God blessed people in that period, so much that I can say, without fear, that God was closer to humans in the ancient world than he is today.

One might ask, "Why are you saying so? There were not many hospitals, not many nutritional advisers, not much drinking water, and not many good houses because money was very hard to come by."

Yet life was very good. When you heard that someone was dead, it generally was because he or she was old.

There were no good roads. There were no telephones, but they were able to communicate very well. How did the slaves working on their masters' plantations communicate with each other? God gave them the wisdom of communication and understanding.

There were few educated people, but they were able to do things very well at their understanding. They were economists who practiced economics at their own level, and it worked well. They were able to balance their accounts well but never went to school. You rarely hear of financial misappropriation among them because they feared the gods they served.

There was no electricity, and there were no refrigerators, yet they were able to preserve their farm products and other foods very well. There were no pressing irons, but they ironed their clothes. We might wonder how they did that.

The disadvantage they had was when there was an outbreak of disease or when there was an emergency need of something.

It was a period when children were trained to respect their elders, and a child's behavior outside the home was measured by the house from which that child came. There was easy identification of individuals. Few were educated, but they were rich in knowledge of how to do things. We might wonder who taught them and how they made it.

The world was far apart, meaning that to travel from one town to another took days of walking barefoot. The only things you could see were the trees. The voices you heard were from the birds and sounds from the trees.

It was a period when humans lived in poverty. People were sold or were sent to serve the creditors of their parents or the family heads to offset their debts.

The traditional priests were the kings of the towns, and they dictated the fate of the people because few religious groups were known.

Community gatherings were beautiful. People were friendly at Richard's house, not far from Eric's house. Friends' wives cooked, and they all sat down and ate from one bowl. Life was at its best.

THE PRESENT-DAY WORLD

In today's twenty-first-century world, people say the world is a global village. What does this imply? You can call someone in a different country and talk as if he or she was standing next to you. Your bank account is at your fingertips. You can work from home.

This is the period that Revelation 11:7–10 talks about:

> And when they finish their testimonies, the beast that ascends out of the bottomless pit, will make war against them, overcome them, and kill them. And their dead bodies will lie in the street of the great city, which spiritually is called Sodom and Egypt, where also, our lord was crucified. then those from the peoples tribes, tongues, and Nations will see their dead

bodies three and half days and not allow their dead bodies to be put into graves. And those who dwell upon on earth will rejoice over them, make merry, and send gifts one to another, because these two prophets tormented those who dwelt on the earth.

This prophecy of John has not yet come to pass, but this should give us an idea of what is about to happen. Today, nothing is hidden, and nowhere is too far from where you are. All that we did not see in the ancient world is here today.

It is also called the technological or scientific world. Whatever you want to know or to learn is right at your fingertips. Go to the computer or your phone, and it is done.

Those who are computer-literate are the most vondriable people to the devil on this planet. Lucky you if you have a child, a brother, a sister, or a close friend who knows how to use a computer or other technology; otherwise, I am sorry for you.

This is a period in which respect for the elderly has died, and humans have no trace of where they came from—the tribe or the home. People do anything and behave any way, without looking back. What a pity that is, yet we don't see it.

Is social media making life better for the world or worse, especially for the young up-and-coming in our communities?

4

THE OBVIOUS CHANGES IN THE WORLD

Let's look at some changes in the world that should give Christians a heads-up about what can happen soon and at any time. These change some from positive to negative and some from negative to positive—all in the name of fun.

Years ago in Ghana, you could see young boys and girls playing together naked between the ages of fifteen and sixteen, without any ill feelings or shyness. In those days, when your sister began menstruating, the family would perform customs and rites for her to usher her into womanhood. That used to show great respect to the sister and to the family, and all could see that the sister was really mature. From then on, her manner of dress and attitude changed, as well as her speech.

She previously had been talked to, but now she commanded respect.

Today, when you learn that a twelve-year-old girl is pregnant, you hear, "Oh my goodness! What happened? When did she begin menstruating, and what did the family do for her before she became pregnant? What does she know about herself, and what can she do for herself?"

Things that we used to refer to as taboo (or that the Bible called taboo) are today seen as happening in the name of having fun or being one's right.

My mother told me that she realized I had become a man when she noticed that my voice had become deep. She called me early one morning and told me, "My son, you are now a man. I don't want some parents to wake me up from my sleep because they have something to discuss with me. They might say, 'We have noticed our daughter is pregnant. When we asked her who is responsible, she mentioned your son. So, we are here to inform you about it.' No, please, if you don't want to finish school but want to be a father, and you see any lady of your choice, bring her home and introduce her to me, and let's take it from there."

Not long ago, I saw on national television and on social media something of which you will bear witness. On the streets of the UK and Germany, naked men and women—a lot of them—were riding bicycles. What is going on? They were having fun.

Today, an hour seems like ten or twenty minutes when we

are celebrating Christmas; the other one is also at the corner, waiting, and in no time, it's here.

The time has passed when it was a taboo to go fishing with chemicals, for they said it would pollute the waters, but today, it's the best way to fish.

Is there any sense in what I am talking about here? Is there anything to learn from this? God have mercy on us.

The Reasons for God's Creation

The question is this: has God really achieved the purpose for which he created the world?

Is the world under God's control? Jesus addressing his disciples by saying, "Here comes the ruler of the world," which really affirms the question.

This statement calls for critical thinking and the help of the Holy Spirit to understand what it means.

> And the devil taking him up into an high mountain, showed unto him all the kingdom of the world in a moment of time. and the devil said unto him all these powers will I give these, and the glory of them for that is delivered unto me and to whomsoever I will give it. if thou therefore wilt worship me all shall be thine. (Luke 4:5–7)

Now is the judgment of this world. Now the
ruler of this world will be cast out. (John 12:31)

Can you see this world? This is a period in which religious
groups have sprung up more than ever. The love of money and
fame is on the increase. Wickedness is the order of the day.
There is no respect for human life at all.

No wonder the fake pastors and so-called prophets
speak with so much authority and walk with their chests out,
deceiving many through distortion, all because of worldly
things, forgetting that tomorrow they may die.

The fear of God is diminishing quickly. It's very hard to
find a true love, if there is anything called love at all. Instead,
it's about money and fame.

This world has passed through the dispensation of God the
Father, when God appeared to humankind and when he wanted
to speak to man face-to-face. After that came the dispensation
of God, the Son. That was the period of Jesus Christ, who
appeared as a human—fully man and fully spirit.

That which was from the beginning which we
have heard which we have seen with our eyes
which we have looked upon and our hands
have handled of the word of life—the life
was manifested and we have seen it, and bear
witness and shew unto you that eternal life
which was with the father and was manifested
unto us, that which we have seen and heard,

declare we unto you that ye also may have fellowship with us and truly our fellowship is with the father and with his son Jesus Christ. (1 John 1:1-3)

Redeeming the Time

Looking at the time in which we find ourselves now, is there anything to think of?

> See then that you walk circumspectly, not as fools but as wise redeeming the time because the days are evil. Therefore do not be unwise but understand what the will of the Lord is. (Ephesians 5:15–17)

Again, what is happening of which we must be in the know? On a serious note, has this world ever been destroyed? If yes, what was the cause? Can it happen again?

> At that time, Michael would stand up. The great prince who stands watch over the sons of your people and she'll be in a time of trouble such as never was since the throne was a nation. Even to that time and at that time your people shall be delivered. Everyone whose name will be found written in the book of life, and many

of those who sleep in the dust of the earth shall awake some to everlasting life some to shame and everlasting contempt.

Those who are wise shall shine like the brightness of the firmament and those who turn many to righteousness like the stars forever and ever. But you Daniel shut up the words and seal the book until the time of the end many shall run to and fro and knowledge shall increase. Then I, Daniel, looked and there stood two others one on this riverbank and the other on that river bank and said to the man clothed in linen who was above the waters of the river how long shall the fulfillment of these wonders be? (Daniel 12:1–6)

Consider the following questions:

1. We know that this world has gone through transformations before. Can you think of anything that calls for that?
2. Can you relate any of those courses to the happenings of today's world?
3. What is an emergent church and its contemplative prayers? Is there anything called *true Christian* that one has to consider?
4. What is a CRISPR Cas device (meaning and its explanation)?

5. What do we know about the train line linking southern and northern Europe in Switzerland? It was opened in June 2016. How was the opening ceremony performed?
6. What is the history of Mount Graham in Arizona, USA?
7. What is transhumanism? Is there any history behind it and anything we can learn from it now?
8. Does the world of today have a seer—someone who sees things that are about to happen and advises on them?

Now the king of Syria was making war against Israel and he consulted with his servants saying my camp will be in such a place and the man of God sent to the king of Israel saying "Beware that you do not pass this place for the Syrians are coming down there"

Then the king of Israel sent someone to the place of which the man of God had told him. Thus he warned him and was watchful there not once or twice. Therefore the heart of the King of Syria was greatly troubled by these things and called his servants and said to them, "Will you not show me which of us is for the King of Israel?" And one of his servants said, "None my Lord O, King but Elisha the prophet who is in Israel tell the King of Israel the words that you speak in your bedroom" (2 Kings 6:8–12)

5

THE CHURCH

Can you help me sing this song?
The church is marching on
The church is marching on
And the gate of hell shall not prevail
The church is marching on
And the gate of hell shall not prevail
The church is marching on

Is the church of today marching on spiritually or physically or materialistically? Some people have the perception that the God of today's church is different from the God of the early believers' church. This is due to the attitude and approach that these two generations show. What can you, as a Christian of today, say?

What Is a Church, After All?

The word *church* was first mentioned in Matthew 16, when Jesus wanted to know what the people were saying about him. Here, we see Peter's revelation about the Master Jesus.

> Jesus answered and said to him blessed are you Simon, Bar Jonah for flesh and blood has not revealed this to you but my father who is in heaven. And I also say to you that you are Peter and upon this rock, I will build my church and the gates of hades shall not prevail against it. (Matthew 16:17–18)

Take note that Peter was called Simon Bar Jonah, but Jesus tells him that from today, he is Peter, and on this rock (meaning upon this confession) Jesus will establish his name. There are other Jesuses in the Bible, but our Jesus is the Son of God and has "the Christ" attached to his name (*Christ* means "the anointed one"). It is only those in the Spirit who can call on Christ. If I may ask, are you still Josephine or Eric or Jackson, by which people know you?

> Do not be conformed to this world but be transformed by the renewing of your mind. That you may prove what is that good and acceptable and perfect will of God. (Romans 12:2)

And he was saying Because of this I have said to you that no one is able to come to me unless it shall have been granted to him from the father. (John 6:65 Berean Literal Bible)

Theologians say that the words *I will build my church* indicate that the church has not yet been started. Obviously, the disciples did not understand the doctrine of the New Testament at this point. The disciples' understanding at the time was that they were the Lord's followers.

So who is to form the church, and how is it going to be? Is the church going to be visible or invisible?

Therefore remember that formerly you who were Gentles the birth and called "uncircumcised' by those who call themselves 'the circumcision' (which is done in the body by human hands) remember that at that time, you were separate from Christ excluded from citizenship in Israel, and foreigners to the covenants of the promise without hope and without God in the world. But now, in Christ Jesus you who once were far away have been brought near by the blood of Christ. (Ephesians 2:11–13 NLT)

The gates of Hades shall not prevail against it. Jesus may have been saying that death would not vanquish the church by the power of his Resurrection one day. The church—all the redeemed—will be resurrected. This is the assumption of some theologians, but others say that the phrase means that the forces of evil will not be able to conquer the people of God.

My understanding of the two statements is that the word *redeem* can also mean those who have been saved from the world or called out of the traditions, cultures, tribes, languages, and nations into his marvelous kingdom by believing that Jesus Christ is the Son of the most high God. He indeed is the Lord of the world, and we confess him as such.

Then let's consider our father Abraham, who was called by God to come out of his country, out of his father's house, and from his people, even though he had not seen God but just obeyed the call. He left with his father, wife, and nephew. Abraham did not ask questions; he simply obeyed and believed that God was real and that he would surely lead him to a better place.

The word *church* is from the Greek word *ekklesia*, meaning "a called-out assembly." The church can also mean an assembly of people with a common faith and understanding, pursuing a common goal.

I can boldly say a church is built on believing, confession of faith, and obeying the Word of God.

The Church in the Wilderness

Let's consider also the church in the wilderness of Israel and how God redeemed his people from Egypt to worship him. This shows how unique these people were to God. His presence with them in the wildness—that is how you and I, who have come to believe in his Son, are to him.

> Afterword Moses and Aaron went in and told Pharaoh, thus says the Lord God of the Israel let my people go that they may hold a feast to God in the wildness and Pharaoh said who is the Lord that I should obey him to let the people of Israel go? I do not know the Lord nor will I let Israel go. (Exodus 5:1–2)

God eventually prevailed to deliver the Israelites to the promised land.

But the church of the Lord has not come on an easy route. People labeled them as rebellious people, and they suffered violence from the people they lived with.

All kinds of situations that are not mentioned happened to them, all in the name of the church to come.

The Early Church

The Israelites did not have it easy, coming out of Egypt. Remember the apostle Paul coming out of his own people.

> Now, when they had passed through Amphipolis and Apollonia, they came to

Thessalonica where there was a synagogue of the Jews. Then Paul as his custom was, went into them and for three Sabbaths reasoned with them from the scriptures explaining and demonstrating that the Christ had to suffer and rise again from the dead, and saying this Jesus whom I preach to you is the Christ. And some of them were persuaded and a great multitude of the devout Greeks and not a few of the leading women joined Paul and Silas. But the Jews who were not persuaded became envious, took some of the evil men from the marketplace and gathered a mob to set all the city in an uproar and attack the house of Jason and sought to bring them out to the people But, when they did not find them. They dragged Jason and some brethren to the rulers of the city, crying out that those who have turned the world upside down have come here too. (Acts 17:1–6)

Nevertheless even among the rulers many believed in him but because of the Pharisees they did not confess Him lest they should be put out of the synagogue. For they love human praise more than praise from God. (John 12:42–43)

This has been the situation of the church from the times of old until today. Many people have been killed in a violent manner. Some have left their homes, running to unknown places, just as it happened in Acts 9, when the disciples were running away out of fear of being persecuted after Saul obtained letters to pursue them, arrest them, and jail them.

The church is you and I, those of us who have accepted Jesus Christ as their Lord and Savior. Christ says he will come for his church as a bride for the bridegroom, without spot or wrinkle. The church is not the building, as some think and believe. Christ is not coming for the building but for those redeemed and transformed by renewing their minds. That is why we must watch our steps and our attitudes with one another.

The Christ in you is the hope of your glory. May the Lord be with you and with all those who have come to believe.

What do you think is the expectation of the world from the church? Remember that you are the salt and the light of this world. Those to whom much is given, much is expected.

Now let's go into the history of the church.

The church of the Dark Ages (also called the Early Middle Ages) was the only church in those days, and that church was the Roman Catholic Church. What was the state of the church at that time? People stood against reason of knowledge.

Later came Martin Luther, a German monk who forever changed Christianity. He wrote his Ninety-Five Theses and posted them on a church door in 1517, sparking the Protestant

Reformation, which brought in the Church of England (the Anglican Church) and the church of America, the Methodist Church.

When the first president of the Republic of Ghana, Dr. Kwame Nkrumah, called Pastor James McKeown, the founder of the Church of Pentecost, to question him on what he had done for the people of Ghana, Pastor McKeown's answer was, "I have a message that is changing the lives of the bad ones in the society, making them responsible people in their communities." The president was overjoyed and congratulated the pastor and asked him to go ahead with his good works.

The church must be the light to the communities in which we live and to the people around us. Be an example to people at your workplace and anywhere you find yourself. The character of the church must be a force to be reckoned with.

How can the church overturn the decisions of our societies, tribes, or clans? This is a very important question, but that was why Jesus said, "And I will give you the keys of the kingdom of heaven and whatever you loose on earth will be loose in heaven. And whatever you bind on earth will be bind in heaven" (Matthew 16:19).

As soon as you accept Christ as your Lord and Savior, the first thing you will need from God is the power from above, which is your key. Jesus Christ promised the church that when he comes upon you, you will be courageous, and he will teach you all things. He said he will take from him to you, as was said of John and Peter. These were not the people we know as fishermen. They never went to school, but they spoke with power and authority.

> In him you trusted, after you heard the word of truth, the gospel of your salvation in whom also having believed, you were sealed with the Holy spirit of promise. (Ephesians 1:13)

Any important letter without a seal does not have much value. The seal means it is complete and from an authority.

CHRIST'S LIFE AND RESURRECTION

The birth, life, and Resurrection of Jesus, the living God, is the center of Christianity. Christ's Resurrection gives a new hope, reaffirming his words when he was alive and proving his power over all things in the heavens and on earth or beneath.

Christ's Resurrection overshadows the power of the sun god, and it is absolutely right for Christians to meet on this day to worship him to show his supremacy to all the earth and in the heavens.

No one rejoices when his or her beloved child, friend, or other family member is killed, suffering a painful death, without knowing what that person did wrong. But upon hearing of his Resurrection, all these people have every cause to rejoice and to worship his authority over death and the hope he brought back.

> Rejoice with those who are rejoicing and weep
> with those who are weeping. (Romans 12:15)

Pentecost means the feast of fifty for the Israelites in Acts 2. It was on this day that the Holy Ghost fell upon the disciples, and it was on this fateful day that God gave a platform to the apostle Peter when people from all walks of life gathered together in Jerusalem to celebrate the festival.

> There were dwelling in Jerusalem Jews, devout
> men from nation under heaven and when this
> sound occurred the multitude came together,
> and were confused because everyone heard
> them speak in his own language. (Acts 2:5–6)

> But Peter, standing up with the eleven, raised
> his voice and said to them, men of Judea and
> all who dwell in Jerusalem, let this be known
> to you, and heed my words. For these are not
> drunk, as you suppose. since it is only the third
> hour of the day. But this is what was spoken by
> the prophet Joel. (Acts 2:14–16)

> Men of Israel hear these words: Jesus of
> Nazareth, a man attested by God to you by
> miracles, wonders and signs which God did
> through him in your midst, as you yourselves
> also know. Him being delivered by the

determined purpose and foreknowledge of God, you have been taken by lawless hands and have been crucified and put to death. Whom God raised up having loosed the pains of death, because it was not possible that he should be held by it for David says concerning him, I foresaw the Lord always before my face for he is at my right hand that I may not be shaken. (Acts 2:22–25)

Therefore let all the house of Israel know assuredly that God has made this Jesus whom you crucified both Lord and Christ.

Now when they heard this they were cut to the heart and said to Peter and the rest of the Apostles men and brethren, what shall we do?

Then Peter said to them repent and let every one of you be baptized in the name of Jesus Christ for remission of sins and you shall receive the gift of the Holy Ghost for the promise is to you and to your children and to all who are afar off as many as the Lord our God will call. (Acts 2: 36–39)

On this day, three thousand souls were won for Christ. Who can argue why God used that day through Peter to win those souls? Would there be an argument if that day is remembered and observed for the great miracle God did through these fishermen—these people who, according to the scripture, had no education?

What Is the Anchor of Your Church?

An anchor is a device for securing a vessel underwater, holding the vessel in place and giving it stability.

What is the basic belief of your church, and how did it work or inspire the people of old, as compared to contemporary believers? How does it work with other churches of Bible-believing people?

> All scripture is given by inspiration of God and is profitable for doctrine for reproof, or correction, for instruction in righteousness that the man of God may be complete, thoroughly equipped for good work. (2 Timothy 3:16–17)

Can we consider these principles as the anchor for the early church? I know that all Jesus Christ–believing churches believe in these principles, but there is something unique about every church.

The Roman Cathodic Church has this basic principle or belief. Holy Communion and baptism are important to the Anglican Church. The Methodist Church has its roots in the eighteenth century from Anglicanism. It became known as the Holy Club and then the Methodist Church, due to the methodical way of doing things. The church believes in praising God in singing and association of believers.

The Church of Pentecost is known for its salvation message and the power of the Holy Ghost. As the founder said to then-president of the Republic of Ghana, Dr. Kwame Nkrumah, "My message is changing the bad ones in the communities to be responsible people of the communities."

Churches seem to have other things in common, but these things are unique from one to another. The problem here is with the youth, who are taking the mantle from their aging fathers and mothers who do not know the history of the church or the unique beliefs of the churches, by which they should live. These churches seem to be taking a new turn from that which they used to know.

7

THE CITIES OF REFUGE

When God redeemed the Israelites from Egypt, and they were on their way to the promised land, God spoke to Moses, saying, "When you get to the land that I am going to give you, set some cities aside for refuge." These cities were named in the Priestly Code.

> The Priestly Code is the name given by academia to the body of laws expressed in the Torah which do not form part of the Holiness Code, the Covenant Code, the Ritual Decalogue, or the Ethical Decalogue. The Priestly Code constitutes the majority of Leviticus, as well as some of the laws expressed in Numbers.[3]

---

[3] "Priestly Code," Wikipedia, https://en.wikipedia.org/wiki/Priestly_Code.

The Priestly Code states that if someone kills his brother, he must be killed as well at the altar.

> Speak to the children of Israel and say unto them when ye come over Jordan into the land of Canaan, Then ye shall appoint you cities to be cities of refuge for you; that the slayer may flee thither which killed any person at unawares. And they shall be unto you for refuge from the avenger that the manslayer dies not until he stands before the congregation in judgment. And of these cities which ye shall give, six cities shall ye have for refuge. (Numbers 35:10–13)

> Then the Lord spoke to Joshua, saying speak to the children of Israel, saying appoint for yourselves cities of refuge which I spoke to you through Moses, that the slayer who kills a person accidentally or unintentionally may flee there and they shall be your refuge from the avenger of blood. And when he flees to one of those cities, and stands at the entrance of the gate of the city and declares his case in the hearing of the elders of the city they shall take him into the city as one of them and give him a place that he may dwell among them. If the avenger of blood pursues him they shall not deliver the slayer into his hand because he

struck his neighbor unintentionally, but did not hate him beforehand.

And he shall dwell in that city until he stands before the congregation for judgment and until the death of the one who is high priest in those days. Then the slayer may return and come to his own city. and his own house to the city from which he fled.

And they appointed Kedesh in Galilee in the mountains of Naphtali. Shechem in the mountains of Ephraim, and Kirjath Arba (which is Hebron) in the mountains of Juda And on the other side of the Jordan by Jericho eastward, they assigned Bezer in the wilderness on the plain from the tribe of Reuben Ramoth in the Gilead, from the tribe of Gad and Golan in Basham from the tribe of Manasseh. These were the cities appointed for the children of Israel for the stranger who dwelt among them that whoever killed a person accidently, might flee there and not die by the hand of the avenger of blood until he stood before the congregation. (Joshua 20:1–9)

God, being a man of justice, was not cultivated from anywhere but is of him. As he was from the beginning, so he is today.

What can we say of the New Testament? Jesus said, "Come unto me all ye that labor and are heavy laden and I will give rest" (Matthew 11:28). Jesus receives people who are trouble and who are being pursued in the world.

Do you know anyone who has accepted Jesus as his or her Lord and personal Savior? Their lives are bound for the church; it is a refuge to those who were troubled in the world.

In these cities of refuge, the elders were charged with taking care of the refugees—giving them food and clothing and attending to all other needs. They were even protected from their avengers, who could not enter the city. The refugee was not allowed to go back while the priest was alive.

Can it be said of the church today that the elders of the church will take care of people who have no help and nowhere to turn and will supply the needs of such people without judging them or reminding them of what brought them there? Would they not give up these people to their avengers when they are being searched for?

I know of a man who was accused of being a witch when he was a child. A prophetess from his mother's church told the mother, who was a rival to the so-called prophetess, that her son was a witch. Because the mother was going through hard times (which had brought her into the church), she believed the prophetess. And then his siblings heard of it, which was a sad story for the innocent boy.

This boy was the last born of nine siblings; four had already passed away. His brothers did not take kindly to him at all.

When the mother's rival prophesied that the boy was a witch, they gave him all kinds of cruel treatment that he deserved as a witch.

When an older brother's wife passed away, the boy was accused of being the one who had killed the woman. Not a single day passed without his receiving bad treatment. Life was very rough for this innocent boy.

Another brother was chasing someone's wife, and the husband cursed him. He became sick, and the boy was accused of being the cause. One evening, his sick brother asked him to go with him to the farm, which was close to the village. This innocent boy followed his brother, not knowing what he had planned—the brother was going to kill him at the farm to end their problems. Is it not sad that people don't want to take responsibility for their own lives and blame others for their failures?

On reaching the farm, they met a hunter on a hunting expedition. He asked them, "What are you doing here at this time of day?"

The older brother answered, "We are coming for some food."

The hunter then said, "Hurry up, then, and leave, for it is too late in the evening for you to be here." He then asked, "Do you people know me?"

The older brother answered, "No, sir."

And to their surprise, the hunter said, "You are my children."

The younger boy never knew his father; he had passed away when the boy was three months old.

The hunter waited for the boys to finish whatever they were there to do, and then he followed them to the village close to their house and gave them a message for their mother before he left them.

Days and months passed before the older brother told another brother what he had planned to do to this poor boy and then what had happened.

God, in the heavens, knew the heart of the young boy— that he was innocent—and sent a hunter to save his life.

Today, this boy is the breadwinner for the entire family. God has blessed him. He is living in the United Kingdom.

This testimony is to let you know that when someone is in a state of frustration, anything that will take away his or her frustration is OK, without considering the aftermath results

Many have gone through situations such as this; some are in it right now.

God has set the nation of America aside as a land of refuge for the whole world. The forefathers knew that God loved Israel, as he loved the nation of America, and blessed it. Do you consider it a mistake for America to have such a unique relationship with Israel? Even the US Constitution seeks to protect anyone who sets his or her feet on the land of America. It was not by mistake that those who drafted the Constitution were inspired by the Spirit of God.

Are immigrants protected by the US Constitution? The brief answer is yes. When it comes to key constitutional provisions, like due process and equal treatment under the law, the US Constitution applies to all persons, both documented undocumented, and not just US citizens. Let me remind you of the Pilgrims' progress. Who were they?

Today, the American nation is in the state of King Nebuchadnezzar's dream, in which he saw an image, tall and strong, but the underpart was clay mixed with iron. This is where America is now, and if care is not taken, America will fall the most.

Today, if those in government would do away with politics and respect the laws concerning strangers, receiving them and caring for them as it was from the beginning of the nation of America, no other nation could compare itself to America, for the living God will be its provider and protector, as he said, "And I myself will be a wall of fire around it declare the Lord and I will be its glory within" (Zechariah 2:5 NIV).

Right now, the nation of North Korea has become a thorn in the flesh of America and its allies, as Goliath became a thorn in the flesh of the Israelites. I declare and decree today that if America will accept the shortfall of this nation and go back to its laws of old, what David did to Goliath will happen to North Korea in no time, not by might or power but by my spirit of the Lord. So said the prophet in Zechariah 4:6. It can also be said of these nations, when talking about Christianity, that American cannot be ruled out.

Let me tell you of something unique—the Azusa Street Revival, which started in 1906 and ended in 1915. It was started by a small group of black Americans holding a revival, led by William J. Seymour, in Los Angeles, California. The Holy Spirit took over the program, and the people spoke in tongues. This revival was historic.

The small country of Ghana in Africa has great fortunes. Some call Ghana the gateway to Africa, without knowing what they are talking about. It used to be called the Gold Coast, but that was changed to Ghana by the first president, Dr. Kwame Nkrumah, a great man with great energy and wisdom. No Africa president in history has been able to match his accomplishments.

After that, he went to Egypt, and he came back with very high energy. Just a few people around him knew of it as he built his country. If the preceding governments had left it up to people's expectations and to the satisfaction of Ghana, the country would have been highly respected with dignity.

As of this writing, Ghana has Nana Addo Dankwa Akufo-Addo as the president, who has a different dimension of energy, which comes with the name Nana. If people will have patience and pray for him, what God wishes for the country will come to realization during his term in office.

The coming of Nana Akufo-Addo to the seat of presidency has changed the spiritual dimensions of the country. The name *Nana* is of royal descent, which has a very high influence. Jesus called his followers *royals* before calling them *the priesthood*.

People must watch out for Ghana during Akufo-Addo's presidency. The firstborn blessing for the country will begin to unfold, which is the evidence of the firstborn of Africa, as God called Israel *my firstborn* and blessed them. So Ghana will be to the African continent.

Nana Addo Dankwa Akufo-Addo's record will be very hard to reckon with by any African president, if not the size of his government, but the real Ghana, the gateway to Africa, will soon be seen.

WHAT DOES GOD KNOWS ABOUT YOUR CHURCH?

The Loveless Church

To the angel of the church of Ephesian write. These things say He who holds the seven stars in his right hand, who walks in the midst of the seven golden lampstands. I know your works, your labor, your patience, and that you can not bear those who are evil. And you have tested those who say they are Apostles and are not and have found them. Liars and you have persevered and have patience, and have labored for My name's sake and have become weary,

Nevertheless I have this against you that you have left your first love. Remember therefore from where you have fallen repent and do the first works or else I will come to you quickly and remove your lampstand from its place unless you repent

But you have that you hate the deeds of the Nicolaitans which I also hate.

He who has an ear let him hear the spirits of the churches. To him who overcomes I will give to eat from the tree of life which is in the midst of paradise God. (Revelation 2:1-7)

The Persecuted Church

And to the angel of the church in Smyran write,

These things say the First and the Last, who was dead and came back to life. I know your work's tribulation and poverty [but you are rich] and I know the blasphemy of those who say they are Jews and are not but are a synagogue of Satan. Do any of those things which you are about to suffer. Indeed the devil. Is about to throw some of you into prison that may be tested and you will have tribulation for ten days. Be faithful until. Death and I will give you the crown of life.

He who has an ear let him hear what the spirit says to the churches. He who overcomes shall not hurt by the second death. (Revelation 2:8–11)

The Compromising Church

And to the angel of the church in Pergamos write

These things say He who has the sharp two end sword. "I know your works and where you dwell where Satan 's. thrown is. And you hold fast to my name and did not deny my faith even in the days in which Antipa was my faithful martyr who was killed among you where Satan dwells. But I have a few things against you, because you have those who taught Balak to put a stumbling block before the children of Israel to eat things sacrificed to idols and to commit sexual immorality. Thus you also have those who hold the doctrines of the Nicolaitans which I hate. Repent or I will come to you quickly and I will fight against them with the sword of my mouth.

Let he Who has an ear let him hear what the spirit says to the churches. To him who overcomes it I will give some of the hidden manna to eat and I will give him a white stone, and on the stone a new name written which no one knows except him who receives it. (Revelation 2:12–17)

Compromising in certain situations can be good or bad, depending on the context in which the situation falls.

The uncertain situation of Christianity today has come about due to compromise. Esau compromised with his brother Jacob to sell his birthright to him because he was dying of hunger. But a time came when Esau realized that being the firstborn was important and a blessing. The Bible says he sought his right, but it was too late.

The crisis in Christianity today has come about due to compromises here and there. Joshua and his able men compromised with men from a country that God had told them to destroy and everything within it. They came to Joshua, claiming they had come from a far country. They showed their bread, which was very old, and their sandals. He had compassion for them and signed a covenant with them that when the Israelites got to their country, they would be their slaves and serve them. Just after that, Joshua and his men realized that they were the next town for which God had told them not to leave a stone unturned. Now, because of the covenant, the Israelites could not so anything but accommodate them.

Christianity has been in compromising situations, and it

has not worked out well for it. Whenever God says, "I hate it," he really hates it, and there is no way that God will change his mind to love it.

The almighty Abraham, who couldn't wait for the promise of God, compromised with his wife to take their maid servant, and today, you and I can attest to the results of it.

Joseph's brothers compromised to kill him because of his dreams but ended up selling him to an Egyptian and told their father that Joseph was dead.

Compromising started during the days of Constantine the Great, when he ruled in Roman Empire. As a great king, he tried to use his influence to seek compromise between the Christians and the idol worshippers so both of them could live in peace. This was from 306 BC to 337 BC. The pagans worshipped the sun god and moon god, like the goddess Diana in Ephesus and Corinth. This situation has haunted the church of God until today.

It is my prayer that as we come to realize the cause of these situations—like the riot of Ephesus in Acts 19, due to the work of the man Demetrius, and the days of Balak and Balaam—we must understand why God strongly warns believers not to compromise in any way

In the Bible, God said, be ye holy for the Lord you God I am holy. He said, come out from among them, and do not be an unequal yoke with them talking about unbelievers.

He asks what the light has to do with darkness. He tells them separate from them and be holy unto their God.

The Corrupt Church

And to the angel of the church in Thyatira write

These things say the son of God who has eyes, like a flame of fire, and His feet like fine brass. I know your works, love, service, faith, and your patience, and as for your works, the last are more than the first.

Nevertheless I have a few things against you because you allow that woman Jezebel, who calls herself a prophesier to teach and seduce my servants to commit sexual immorality and eat things sacrificed to idols.

And I gave her time to repent of her sexual immorality and she did not repent. Indeed I will cast her into a sickbed, and those who commit idolatry with her into great tribulation unless they repent of their deeds. I will kill her children with death and all the churches shall know that I am He who will give to each one of you according to your works.

Now to you I say and to the rest in Thyatira as many do not have this doctrine who have not known the depths of satan as they say I will put on you no other burden.

But hold fast what you have till I come.
And he who overcomes and keeps my works
until the end. To him I will give power over the
nations. (Revelation 2:18–26)

This is an incomprehensible statement. How can one explain this corrupt church?

A story was told about a man who was traveling by ship. Because he didn't know how to swim, he looked for the best swimmer on board and became his friend, sharing whatever he had with him. He did this so that if there was an uncertain situation, his new friend would help him.

In no time, a storm started, and the sea began to toss the ship. The man looked for his friend, the best swimmer on board. He looked everywhere, but his friend was nowhere to be found. Then he went under the deck of the ship, and he found his friend sitting there, crying.

"What is the matter?" he asked.

"I am scared of this kind of storm and sea," his friend answered.

Then this man, who had trusted this so-called best swimmer, thought, *If even the best swimmer is crying, what will I do?*

The Bible says not to put your trust in others but to trust the Lord, your God, in every situation. He will be there for you.

If we should talk about people who are corrupt, let's talk about the politicians.

If we should talk about an institution that is corrupt, let's talk about the education system, the police system, and the insurance companies.

But what about the house of God? Were the pastors selling anointing oil from Israel or salt from the Dead Sea or selling consultations? Should I consider sowing a seed on every occasion?

The apostle Paul said certain things must not be mentioned about the church and believers, for they represent God.

Many churches like these have put individuals into psychological situations, and many families are devastated. People have died prematurely.

The Dead Church

And to the angel of the church in Sardis writer, these things say He who is the seven spirit of God and the seven stars. I know your works, that you have a name that you are alive, but you are dead.

Be watchful and strengthen the things which remain, that are ready to die for I have not found your works perfect before God. Remember therefore how you received and heard: hold fast and repent, therefore if you will not watch, I will come upon you

You have a few names even in Sardis who have not defiled their garments and they shall walk with Me in white for they are worthy. He who overcomes shall be clothed in his name from the book of life; but I will confess his name before my father and before His angels. He who has an ears let him hear what the spirit says to the church. (Revelation 3:1–6)

Dead church? Which church is this prophecy going for today—your church or my church? What will make the church, which is the body of God, either dead or alive?

As the apostle Paul said in Ephesians 5:17, do not quench the spirit but be spiritually minded, singing hymns and psalms to glorify the name of the Lord because the Spirit keeps the church alive. The book of Romans 8:5–6 says,

For they that after the flesh do mind the things of the flesh but they that are after the spirit, do mind the things of the spirit for to be carnally minded is death but spiritually minded is life and peace. (KJV)

Sampson lost his strength, but he thought it was there, so when the Philistines were coming, he said, "I will wake up and shake myself as I used to do." But when he woke up, he realized that his strength was gone, and he had become an ordinary man.

Take a critical look at your church and compare it today and in years past—is it alive, dead, or dying?

It seems we put our time into learning theological terms and seasons and in building types of buildings. Souls are coming, but the spiritual strength of the church is not like it was before. Why?

I had a chat with a bishop who is a charge of a particular church, and this is what he said: "We see it and feel it but those in charge of affairs don't see it that way, so if you say it, you become a target."

Pastors are scared of themselves. No wonder Apostle Paul rebuked Apostle Peter for being a hypocrite. The apostle Peter said that if within a time, a moment, a twinkle of an eye, heaven and earth and all other things would be no more, what manner of persons should we be? And what kind of churches should we have?

The Faithful Church

And to the angel of the church in Philadelphia write. These things says He who is holy He who is true, "He who has the keys of David. He who opens and no one can shuts and shuts and no one can opens"

"I know your works, see I have set before you an open door and no one can shut it: for you have a little strength, have kept my word, and have not denied my name. Indeed I will make those of the synagogue of Satan who say they are Jews and are not, but lie – I deed I will make them come and worship before your feet, and to know that I have loved you.

Because you have kept my command to preserve: I also will keep you from the hour of trial which shall come upon the whole world. To test those who dwell on the earth. Behold I am coming quickly. Hold fast what you have that no one may take your crown.

He who overcomes I will make him a pillar in the temple of my God and he shall go out no more.

I will write on him the name of my God and the name of the city of my God, the new Jerusalem which comes down out of heaven from my God. And I will write to him my new name. He who has ears, let him hear what the spirit says to the church. (Revelation 3:7–13)

The Lukewarm Church

And to the angel of the church of the Laodiiceans write, these things say the Amen the faithful and true witness the beginning of the creation of God.

"I know from your work that you are neither cold nor hot. I wish you were cold or hot. So then because you are lukewarm, and neither cold hot, I will vomit you out of my mouth, because you say I am rich, have become wealthy and have need of nothing and do not know that you are wretched, miserably, poor, blind and naked,

I counsel you to buy from me gold refined in the fire that you may be rich, and white garments that you may be clothed that the shame of your nakedness may not be revealed. And anoint your eyes with eye salve that you may see.

As many as I love, I rebuke and chasten. Therefore be zealous and repent. Behold I stand at the door of your heart and knock, if anyone hears my voice and opens the door I will come in to him and dine with him and he with me.

To him who overcomes I will grant to sit with me on my throne as I also overcame and sat down with my father on his throne.

He who has an ear let him hear what the spirit says to the churches. (Revelation 3:14–22)

As you read about these churches, did many thoughts run through your mind? And for one or two things that crossed your mind, looking at your church, did tears fill your eyes?

What can you do? Please pray that those in authority will come to themselves through the evolution of God so they can make things right before the wrath of God comes.

It is my prayer and wish that all churches will be like the church of Philadelphia—with a little strength, they will be able to hold on to the commands of God.

Do you know the God in whom your church believes? Do you believe your priest, pastor, or prophet?

If Rachel had believed the God of Jacob, who was her husband, she wouldn't have stolen the family's god when Jacob was returning to his family.

> Now Rachel had taken the household idols, put them in the camels saddle and sat on them. And Laban searched all about the tent but did not find them. And she said to her father, let it not displease my lord that I can not rise before you, for the manner of a woman is with me. And he searched for her but did not find the household idols. (Genesis 31:34–35)

If you believe in your church and your pastor, why do you challenge other pastors? What is really important about this church to God?

The church is the real revolution of God himself. Through the church, God has revealed himself to certain individuals and to the world. People have seen God in so many ways and have named him all kinds of names, such as Jehovah Jireh, Jehovah Nissi, Jehovah Shammah, El Elyon, Jehovah Adonai, and El Shaddai. He is identified as the bride betrothed to Christ Jesus, but there are instances where the interpretation of the usage varies from church to church. Most believe that it always refers to the church as the bride.

> I am Jealous of you with godly jealousy. I promised you to one husband to Christ so that I might present you as pure virgin to him. (2 Corinthians 11:2 NLT)

> And to present her, to himself as a radiant church without stain or wrinkle or any other beamish but, holy and blameless. (Ephesians 5:27 NLT)

> Let us rejoice and be glad and give him glory for the wedding of the Lamb has come and his bride has made herself ready. (Revelation 19:7 NLT)

I hope you fully understand from these quotes that you are the church, that you are important to God, and that you owe him your precious life.

9

THE PRIESTHOOD OF BELIEVERS

A priest is a religious leader authorized to perform the sacred rituals of a religion, especially, as a mediatory agent between humans and one or more deities. They also have the authority or power of administer religious rites; in particular, rites of sacrifice to and propitiation of a deity or deities.[4]

Unlike in English, the Latin words *sacerdos* and *sacerdium* are used to refer in general to ministerial priesthood shared by bishops and presbyters. A priest of the regular clergy is commonly addressed with the title *Father* in the Catholic Church and some other Christian churches.

Like Islam and Judaism, it has no clergy in the sacerdotal

---

[4] "Priest," Wikipedia, https://en.wikipedia.org/wiki/Priest.

sense. There is no institution that resembles the Christian priesthood of believers. Islamic religious leaders do not have intermediaries between humankind and God, but they have a process of ordination or sacramental function.

The first priest mentioned in the Bible is Melchizedek, who was a priest of the Most High [God and who officiated for Abraham]. The first priest mentioned of another god is Potipherah, priest of On, whose daughter Asenath married Joseph in Egypt. The third priest to be mentioned is Jethro, priest of the Midians and Moses' father-in-law. The first mention of the priesthood occurs in Exodus 40:15. "And thou shall anoint them as thou did anoint their father [Aaron] that they may minister unto me in the priest office for their anointing shall surely be an everlasting priesthood throughout all generations" (KJV).[5]

This quote is not talking about one person but the whole generation of Aaron, and it explains how Aaron was ordained and why. I believe that these reasons for God choosing a priest, pastor, or an evangelist remain the same: (1) to minister unto

[5] "Priesthood (Ancient Israel)," Wikipedia, https://en.wikipedia.org/wiki/Priesthood_(ancient_Israel)#:~:text=The%20first%20priest%20mentioned%20of,and%20Moses'%20father%20in%20law.

God, (2) to stand between the people of the world and God, and (3) to offer sacrifices unto God.

In Leviticus 21:10–23, God explains who is qualified to be ordained as a priest and the rights he has—meaning what he can do and what he cannot do. From all that we have read, God instituted the office of the clergy, the priest, to be the mouthpiece of God to communicate with humankind.

How perfect did this work in the past, and how it is working today? Hebrews 1:1–3 says that in the past, God spoke to our ancestors through the prophets, at many times and in various ways, but in these last days, he has spoken to us by his Son, whom he appointed heir of all things and through whom he made the universe. The Son is the radiance of God's glory and the exact representation of his being, sustaining all things by his powerful Word.

In the past, God maintained a relationship with humankind through the office of the clergy—meaning that the people of God knew God and walked with God per the instructions of the priest—till the coming of his Son, Jesus Christ.

Today, we talk of a priesthood of believers.

> But you are a chosen generation a royal priesthood, a holy nation, His own special people, that you may proclaim the praise of Him who called you out of darkness into his marvelous light.

Who once were not a people but are now the people of God, who had not obtained mercy but now have obtained mercy. (1 Peter 2:9–10)

This statement put us, who call ourselves believers of Christ Jesus, in the position of priests unto God—we who have received the baptism of the Holy Spirit and who are the representatives of Christ Jesus.

Therefore from now on we regard no one according to the flesh. Even though we have known Christ according to the flesh yet now we know him thus no longer.

Therefore if anyone is in Christ, he is a new creation. Old things have passed away: behold all things have become new.

Now all things are of God, who has reconciled us to himself through Jesus Christ and has given us the ministry of reconciliation, that is that God was in Christ reconciling the world to himself, not imputing their trespasses to them and has committed to us the word of reconciliation.

Now then we are ambassadors for Christ as though God were pleading through us we implore you on Christ's behalf to reconcile to God. (2 Corinthians 5:16–20)

So, you and I have responsibility, as recommended in the book of Leviticus 16:12–13. God told the priest to allow the smoke to cover the altar. Otherwise, he would die. The church has its hope in the priest, and the success of people depends on the priest.

> Then he shall take a censer full of burning coals of fire from the altar before the Lord with his hands full of sweet incense between fine and bring it inside the veil.
>
> And he shall put the incense on the fire before the Lord. That the cloud of incense may cover the mercy seat that is on the testimony, lest he die. (Leviticus 16:12–13)

Is Jesus speaking to humankind today, as he was in the past? Answer this question for yourself. Looking at the situation of the present-day world, is our relationship with God as it was before? What is the world's expectation for the clergy? Do the priests still perform their duties as they were instructed before? Find the answers for yourself since you are a priest to your generation.

Take a critical look at yourself and the pastors and the prophets of today. Are we ready for our children? Consider the kind of knowledge they possess, the kind of books they read, and the kinds of groups of which they are a part. Some claim there is no God and no heaven.

How do you feel when you hear these groups—who are supposed to take over as we fade away—thinking and talking like that?

It brings to mind a question a Sunday school child asked his teacher. The child was not convinced by the answer the teacher gave, based on what he had read from a book. He discussed it with his friends and decided to stop going to church. It took the parents a lot of time, trying and praying to find someone who could get an acceptable answer for him.

You see, if you are a parent of today's generation, and you want your children to follow your religion, this is what you will go through if you are not in good standing with your God.

Second Timothy 3:1–17 clearly declares how knowledge acquired in childhood impacts someone. It says by the end, it gives you assurance to hold on to what you have known from your childhood.

Are our leaders, who have been anointed to lead these churches, prepared to understand how the world is changing and when the prophecies of old will start unfolding, according to the scriptures?

God told Daniel to conceal the vision until the appointed time. When is the appointed time going to be?

> But you Daniel shut up the words and sealed
> the book until the time of the end. Many shall
> run to and fro and knowledge shall increase.
> (Daniel 12:4)

Are there significant signs of this scripture? Look into the atmosphere. What do you see, people of God?

The Covenant of God and a Charge to Noah

> But you must not eat meat that has its lifeblood still in it. And for the lifeblood I will surely demand accounting. I will demand accounting from every animal and from each human being too, I will demand accounting for the life of another human being. (Genesis 9:4–5 NLT)

This is the charge that the Lord God gave to Noah. Does this charge go to Noah alone? I believe that you and I bear the same charge today, a charge to keep at heart and glory to glorify. We have a responsibility on our shoulders.

> I will establish my covenant with you.
> Never again will all life be destroyed by the waters of flood, never again will there be a flood to destroy the earth.
> And God said this is the sign of the covenant 1 am making between me and you and every living creature with you a covenant for generations to come. I have set my rainbow in the clouds and it will be a sign of covenant between me and the earth.

Whenever I bring clouds over the earth and the rainbow appears in the clouds I will remember my covenant between me and you and all living creatures of every kind.

Never again will the waters become a flood to destroy all life.

Whenever the rainbow appears in the clouds I will see it and remember the everlasting covenant between God and all living creatures of every kind on earth.

So, God said to Noah this is the sign of the covenant I have established between me and all life on the earth. (Genesis 9:11–17)

For God to prove himself faithful, he did not make a covenant and just leave it there. He set a sign, showing that if he seemed to go beyond the limit, humankind could question him.

What is the sign of your covenant with God, that if you go beyond, it will remember you?

10

WHAT IS ON YOUR MIND?

Let's see if we have received the spirit of fear or of courage and of a sound mind. Do the scriptures say anything about not being ashamed of the gospel in making decisions, in relation to our beliefs?

I was listening to a renowned apostle of a great church of all standards during an endorsing service for an incoming chairman. The service was well organized and well attended. The sermon presentation was marvelous. In delivering the message, the preacher said that during the tenure of the outgoing chairman, an issue came up, but the executives sat on it. They had long hours of debate on this subject. Then they gave the chairman the opportunity to declare his stand on the issue. The chairman started by quoting some scriptures to support what he was going to say. He would not take much time, he said, for this subject would not become a practice of this great church during his term in office.

The whole place became like cemetery—very quiet. Some were happy; some were not. The question I asked myself was this: is the chairman the oldest among them or the best educated person among all the executives?

And this is what came to my mind again: be courageous. Do not fear them, and do not turn to the left or to the right. Meditate on the Book day and night. If you do so, no man or nation will be able to withstand you.

This is why I am asking you: what is on your mind, and what is before you? Does the church of God have courageous men and women—like Jeremiah, Ezra, or Deborah or even this chairman—to say no to the world and yes to God, even in death? Are you the one, or am I the one?

In no time, our opportunity to do something for the Lord will be taken away from us. Be careful you do not say, "I should have done this or that." The time is now.

May the good Lord have mercy on us.

We have a charge to keep. We have a God to glorify.

Consider this song written by the great hymn-writer Charles Wesley in 1762:

> A charge to keep I have,
> A God to glorify,
> A never-dying soul to save,
> And fit it for the sky.

To serve the present age,
My calling to fulfill;
Oh, may it all my pow'rs engage
To do my Master's will!

Arm me with watchful care
As in thy sight to live,
And now thy servant, Lord, prepare
A strict account to give!

Help me to watch and pray,
And still on thee rely,
Oh, let me not my trust betray,
But press to realms on high.

I believe this song has a lot to teach us on what we, as believers, have to offer to this present age.

THE STATE OF CHRISTIANITY—CONFUSION

I see the state of the so-called church of God as in confusion, all in the name of doctrine. Why? For that matter, all the members are confused. All these doctrines are extracts from the same Bible that we all use, so, again, why?

Christians are divided and confused all over the world. This is what I see as I go around, interacting with people. I think that today, Christians need another Martin Luther, who wrote the Ninety-Five Theses to bring changes in the church of early days.

The orthodox churches have their own beliefs and their way of worshipping God, according to their doctrine, which is from the Bible. Even within these orthodox churches, there are some different beliefs from one to another

The Pentecostals have their own beliefs and way of worshipping God, according to their doctrine, which also is from the Bible.

Then comes the charismatic churches. Whatever the Pentecostals do, they do the opposite. Pentecostals say praise and worship; they come with worship and praise. The Pentecostals say women should cover their heads when going before the Lord. Charismatics say it doesn't matter.

Then comes the mushroom churches, referring to the Bible, and the dress code that God instructed Moses for the priests and the church members.

So many differences in beliefs and worship of God in Christianity.

Some believe in baptism by immersion; others believe in baptism by sprinkling. Some believe in the payment of tithes; some say that is an Old Testament teaching that is not in the New Testament. Some believe if a demon is troubling you, a pastor has to take you to the beach at midnight and bathe you in a spiritual bath. If you can not have a baby as a married woman, the spiritual man has to sleep with you so that you are able to have a baby—all according to their doctrines

Some churches believe in praying in tongues; some don't. They have the same Bible teachings.

When the apostle Paul was addressing the church of Corinth, he said who was Apollos and who was Paul—all about the divisions in the church and counseling them to be one in Christ Jesus. In Jesus's last prayers in John 17, he said, "Father, make them one, as you and I are one." Where are all these sayings and teachings in Christianity today?

We have another church, the Latter-day Saints or the Mormon Church, which claims their founder met God in person. It could be possible that God gave him a book, which is the authentic book of the Bible because the original Bible has been authored many times, and the true Word of God is missing. They say theirs is the only church that Christ Jesus knows today. If Christ should come today to take his own, they will be the ones to go.

The Seventh-day Adventists also say that Christ has one church, which is the Seventh-day Adventist Church. If Christ should come and take his own, they will be the ones.

The Jehovah's Witnesses say that God is not a man to destroy what he has made, so God will not destroy the world, as has been preached by Christians. Rather, he will take out the bad ones from earth and leave the good, and the good ones are those who call themselves Jehovah's Witnesses. They have the belief that you can drink, but don't be intoxicated. The Pentecostals and the charismatics teaching that it is not good for a believer to drink any strong wine, as was said to the mother of Samson because the child she was carrying was full of the Holy Ghost. For that matter, the mother should not drink any kind of strong drink, the same as was said to the mother of John the Baptist.

Proverbs 31 says that it is not good for a king to drink strong wine, but give the strong wine to the one who is ready to perish.

What is the meaning of all this confusion? Are the leaders of all these denominations taking advantage of people because they cannot reason for themselves or have not found the truth themselves?

If Christ should come today, what would be our state? Should we hold on to the grace and the mercy of God the Creator?

Please answer these questions for yourself, and help other people to know the truth.

12

IF WE WAIT UNTIL MORNING

Regain for the church of God its past glory—the glory you knew the church to be when you were a child—and the interest people had in going to church—the zeal, the joy, the enthusiasm and the genuineness of heart in doing things for the Lord—in those days, as compared to today.

The prophet Jeremiah says, I am zealous for the Lord and am ready to die for the Lord. Apostle Paul also said the same thing: I am zealous for the Lord and his works.

I know some people who gave their houses to be converted to church houses for free, out of their love for the work of God.

Remember the authority and respect the church leaders had in issues concerning the country and its citizens? Where is that now?

Let's ask ourselves why the attention and attacks from all religious believers, traditional believers, and all other believers are directed to the Christians and the church of God.

The country of Israel started facing attacks from its neighbors many years ago, yet they are progressing. Why won't Christians and the church prevail? The sad thing that worries me is that some Christian Church buildings have been sold to Muslims and some to drinking bars.

Let's look at the men with leprosy and learn from them:

> Now there are four men with leprosy at the entrance of the city gate. They said to each other "why stay here until we die "if we say we will go into the city, the famine is there and we will die and if we stay here we will die. So let's go over to the camp of the Arameans and surrender. If they appear to us we will live if they kill us then we die.
>
> At dusk they got up and went to the camp of the Arameans when reached the edge of the camp, no one was there for the lord had caused the Arameans to hear the sound of a chariot and horses and great army so that they said to one another the Israel's hired the Hittite and Egyptians kings to attack us. So they got up and fled in the dusk, abandoned their tents and their horses and donkeys there left the camp.

As it was and ran for their lives. The men who had leprosy reached the edge of the camp entered one of the tents and ate and drank. They took silver and goods and clothes and went off and hid them. They returned and entered another tent and took some things from it and hid there also.

Then they said to each other what we are doing is not right. This is a day of good news and we are keeping it to ourselves. If we wait until daylight, punishment will overtake us. Let's go at once and report this to the royal palace. (2 Kings 7:3–9 NLT)

I hope you learned something from the actions of these lepers—the boldness, the courage, and allowing God to use them.

13

CONCLUSION

Remember that you are the light of the world. No one puts on a light and then hides it under the table; it is put on the candle stand for people to see their way. And you are the salt. If salt loses its taste, what will it be good for?

Today, scientists say we are in a sophisticated world. If so, then the people of God must do sophisticated things to win the world for God.

People of today's world love money and fame more than human life. Nothing is more important to people than to make a name for themselves, no matter what it may cost.

The clergy and the church are the hope of the world, so to speak. I believe if these people can stand as the apostles did in time past, then this reckless world and life can be saved, as the apostles stood in good times and in bad times.

When I was a child, I respected and feared three groups of people:

1. Priests. In my village, any time it was announced in the church that the priest was coming on a certain day, a gong had to be beaten to announce it to all the people in the village, so they could prepare for the coming of the priest. Some had to go to the farm to get food that was not just good but the best. They would put it all together to give to the priest, and when they gave it to him, you could see the happiness on their faces. They gave so much respect; even the chief of the village had to come to church because the priest was coming.

2. Teachers. Teachers commanded so much respect that parents would take their children to teachers to discipline them. When a student saw his or her teacher on the street, the student quickly ran home to sleep. When a serious case went to the palace, the headmaster was called to sit in the arbitration. So much respect was accorded to teachers. What do you see today?

3. Police. When the constable or low-ranking officer was sent to fetch you, no words or begging would help you. All they knew was that their superior had said to bring you to him. The policeman in the area, town, or village was highly feared and respected.

What has changed the name, the ranks?

> Be very careful then how you live—not
> as unwise but as wise, making the most of
> every opportunity because the days are evil.
> Therefore do not be foolish but understand
> what the Lord's will is.
>
> —Ephesians 5:15–17 (NIV)

Printed in the United States
by Baker & Taylor Publisher Services